In Sickness and In Health
A Love Story

By Allen
Shoffner

To order additional copies of this book, contact:
Xlibris
1-888-795-4274
www.Xlibris.com
Orders@Xlibris.com

CONTENTS

The images are from original
watercolor paintings.

FRONT COVER: MY SWEETHEART'S ENGAGEMENT PICTURE
NOVEMBER 11, 1953

"IN SICKNESS AND IN HEALTH" IS A TRUE LOVE STORY
ABOUT LONG TERM LOVE AND TEST OF FAITH
IN A HUSBAND'S STRUGGLE WITH THE
LONG TERM ILLNESS OF HIS WIFE.

IN SICKNESS AND IN HEALTH

A LOVE STORY

<u>PREFACE</u>

This is a love story. This is a true story. This is my love story. Many love stories have been told. Some have been told in literature, theater, and other forms of public expression. Other love stories rest untold in the hearts and memories of those who have experienced them. I am sure that many of those love stories are as meaningful to those who have experienced them as the one which I am about to write.   So, why should I think that my love story is worthy of telling? Why would anyone be interested in another love story? Simply because no love story could be more meaningful than the one I will now tell.

I have asked myself why I would write this story about a personal part of my life.   I am writing this story for my family and close friends. I am not writing this story for submission to literary agents or publishers. I do not expect to be rewarded by royalties or literary fame. I will be rewarded if any random reader is inspired by what I write. I will be rewarded if this story helps any caregiver endure the pain of seeing the intellect of a beautiful loved one slowly destroyed by Alzheimer's Disease and Parkinson's Disease. I am rewarded by being able to write this story, which is therapy for my mind, body, and soul.

I am inspired to write this love story by my loved one, who is also my wife and friend. During her sickness, she has helped me love her even more, and her constant spiritual faith has helped me regain mine. I dedicate this story to her.

Allen Shoffner

THE VOW

"Will you love her, comfort her, honor and keep her in sickness and in health, and, forsaking all others, keep you only unto her, so long as you both shall live?"

I said "I will," on December 20, 1953. I placed a gold wedding band on the finger of Edna Lucille Jones, and we pledged our love to each other "till death us do part."

We have been faithful to each other, and now, nearly fifty years later, I love her even more in sickness.

-*-

We first met in November, 1952. I was a fresh graduate out of law school at Vanderbilt University. Edna was a recent graduate of the St. Thomas Hospital School of Nursing, who worked in the hospital and still resided in the nurses' dormitory. We met at the Elliston Place Soda Shop, about midway between the Vanderbilt Campus and St. Thomas Hospital. The Elliston Place Soda Shop is still located there like it was more than fifty years ago. This is where some of the student nurses and Vanderbilt students met to flirt and snack. The only other secular enterainment there was a pin ball machine and a nickel music player. The Elliston Place Soda Shop was really a soda shop, but meats and threes were available. No alcohol beverages were on the menu. While writing this story, I read an item in the morning newspaper reporting the death of Lynn Chandler, the former owner and proprietor of the Elliston Place Soda Shop who founded the Soda Shop in 1939. I remember him and Mr. and Mrs. Harold James, the long time managers of the Soda Shop, standing behind the counter there many times. The Elliston Place Soda Shop is truly a Nashville fixture, also fixed in my memory.

When I first saw Edna Jones, I was attracted by her natural beauty. A warm and compassionate personality radiated from her soft smile and soft voice. I realized then that no one could be more beautiful. I do not know if she then felt I was worthy of her attention. I was not a campus fraternity playboy. I could not afford a Greek fraternity. I was not a celebrity. I was a country farm boy. My physical appearance was not impressive. My stature had been affected by polio in childhood, resulting in a spinal scoliosis which required me to wear back braces in my growth years. I was not sure that my charm was overwhelming either. However, we soon convinced ourselves and each other that we were meant to be with each other. Our courtship was somewhat limited by the curfew enforced by the Catholic Sisters at St. Thomas School of Nursing. My memories still return today to the nurses' dormitory and the hospital, both demolished years ago, where I waited many times at the foot of the majestic marbled spiral stairs in the foyer, for my beautiful loved one to meet me. Our courtship was further limited by limited budgets, and consisted mostly of hot chocolate, cruises down Church Street or around the block, and occasionally short term parking on Hayes Street, sometimes steaming the windows, before coming in for curfew. But true love and the laws of nature overcome all such minor limitations. About a year later we pledged to each other a lifetime of that love.

Marble Staircase
Saint Thomas Hospital 1917

LET ME CALL YOU SWEETHEART

Let me call you Sweetheart
I'm in love with you
Let me hear you whisper
That you love me too
Leave the love light glowing
In your eyes so true
Let me call you Sweetheart
I'm in love with you

Longing for you all the while
More and more
Longing for that sunny smile
I adore
Birds are singing far and near
Roses blooming everywhere
You alone my heart will cheer
You just you

Let me call you Sweetheart
I'm in love with you
Let me hear you whisper
That you love me too
Leave the love light glowing
In your eyes so true
Let me call you Sweetheart
I'm in love with you

Let me call you Sweetheart
I'm in love with you

This simple and beautiful love song was written by Beth Slater Whitson in 1910. The lyric has been called one of the greatest love songs of the Twentieth Century. Beth Slater Whitson died of dementia April 26, 1930, in Nashville at the age of 52. *The Tennessean,* March 1, 2006.

My Loved One,
December 20. 1953

TWO BECOME ONE
"SO THEN THEY ARE NO MORE TWAIN, BUT ONE FLESH"

We were married on December 20, 1953, at a historic Lutheran church, my family's home church in rural Bedford County. This Biblical formula provided by Matthew 19, 6 was written upon our marriage certificate. During our marriage, we added three others into the formula: On November 11, 1954, our first child, Melanie, was born at St. Thomas Hospital. On April 29, 1957, our son, Michael Allen, was born also at St. Thomas Hospital. On June 19, 1959, our daughter, Esther, was born at Bedford County Hospital.

Today, as I looked at Edna's wedding photograph I visualized our wedding again in my memory. I remembered how angelic she was in her bridal gown. No poet could describe how she looked to me or how I felt about her, but I thought of Keat's poem that "beauty is a joy forever; Its loveliness increases, it will never Pass into nothingness." I wondered then and still wonder how God, even with His infinite power and the miracles of His Creation, could create such a beautiful person with such a beautiful intellect to share with me. I now wonder how God could allow this beauty and intellect to be taken away.

When we married, I was twenty-seven. Edna was twenty-two. We had each other, but little money. My limited financial resources were exhausted from tuition and expenses at law school. I had been admitted to practice in March, 1952. I did not have established family or business "connections" for law practice and I was trying to establish a practice in my home county. My income for the first full year of practice was $600.00.

Edna had received her pin as a Registered Nurse at St. Thomas Hospital School of Nursing and commuted each day from our home in Shelbyville to Nashville where she had accepted a position as instructor in pediatrics at St. Thomas School of Nursing. During this same time, Edna helped support her widowed mother and younger brother. During the early years of our marriage, we barely afforded the bare necessities of life, even according to the standards of the early fifties. A refrigerator may not have then been considered a luxury, but we did not have one for awhile until a business friend allowed us to buy one on credit at the rate of $15.00 a month. We may have been poor, but we did not think we were poor. We did not beg and borrowed little. We didn't spend much money on entertainment or social activities. My widowed saintly Mother, helped us in many ways. With God's help, we were able to get through these difficult times and our financial fortunes improved. We never became rich by current standards, but we were able to raise a family and provide our children with college education, but more important teach them to know the difference between right and wrong. In 1960 we built the residence which we still call home. In 1970, we built the office building where I practiced law. Our investments did not make us rich, but we were able to live comfortably. We were able to do these things without compromising our principles, honor, and ethics. We were able later to have an active social life, entertain friends, and participate in church and community activities. We were able to dine together and take short vacations together. In September, 1992, we had the good fortune to go on a trip to the Middle East, including the Holy Land, Greece, Egypt, Turkey, and a cruise on the Aegean Sea, conducted by our Pastor and friend of many years, Richard Smith. My favorite picture on this trip was one taken of us at the Captain's table on the cruise ship, showing Edna's expression of joy on what was one of our favorite times together. I will also always remember the beautiful voice of Jane Galbraith, a voice now silenced by Alzheimer's Disease, singing on the tour bus as we drove along the Valley of the Shadow of Death into Jerusalem.

This is just one of many pleasant memories of our life together.

This love story would not be complete without memorializing two ladies who became part of our family life, helping care for our children with motherly love during their formative years: Annie Eunice (Granny) Tenpenney, and Louise Freeman. Both have passed on to Heavenly rest.

As I look back over our years together, I now realize that ours was not a fair partnership. We both worked hard, we were both faithful to each other and family, we both shared the responsibilities and shared the benefits, I helped, but she invested the time, energy, and devotion that made our married life easier. She was the compassionate and caring Mother for our three children: Carrying them to birth, giving them birth, soothing their fears, watching over them during sickness, healing their emotional and physical hurts, taking them to Boy Scouts, Girl Scouts, dancing lessons, confirmation classes at church, ball games and other school activities, staying awake during their teen age years waiting for them to come home, listening for the dreaded calls in the middle of the night, pulling them out of danger, and helping them through their college years and marriages, and then through another generation of their children. She spent countless hours and days over the years in devoted attention to her parents, brother, and other members of her family, staying by their bedsides during extended terminal illnesses. Edna was never afraid to do the menial or "dirty" jobs. I have seen her come home from work many times with her crisp, white uniform or shoes unavoidably soiled in trying to make others more comfortable. She went to the bedside of patients sick with deadly contagious disease where others feared to tread. She never complained.

She has given me much more love, patience, and compassion than I have deserved. I can not recount the ways. She consoled me when I was depressed. She lifted my spirits during the difficult times. She tolerated me when I came home from the office irritable and impatient. She encouraged me when I was discouraged. She taught me patience, tolerance, and understanding. God has blessed me with good health but she has soothed my physical pains and patched my wounds. She has been with me in sickness and in health. She has comforted me with intimate embraces. She has always been by my side. In 1974, she traveled with me thousands of miles when I campaigned as a candidate for a Justice of the Tennessee Supreme Court. In 1988, when I was president of the Rotary Club, she honored me by making a financial contribution to Rotary International naming me a Paul Harris Fellow in the Rotary campaign to eliminate polio in the world. In 2001, she honored me by joining me at the release and signing of my book, The Authority, at the New Covenant Christian Book Store in Shelbyville. She has honored me in many other ways.

She has been honored in many ways by those who have known her. She taught and clinically trained hundreds of students to become nurses. She taught by example, always insisting on high professional standards, not only in nursing skills but also in conduct, ethics, dress, and performance. She was known as the "mother hen" of the nursing students. She was instructor and responsible for the training of Licensed Practical Nurses for more than twenty years, helping 696 through training and "state boards." In 1982, a student honored her with a gift book in which she had written the following: "With much respect, adoration and love. The only way I can repay you for all the wisdom you passed on to me is to pass it on to others who started like me." On November 8, 1989, she received the Henry Feldhaus, Jr. Memorial Community Service Award, awarded by "The People of Bedford County," "due to her dedication for hands trained to nurse and hearts shown how to care." Her class of 1992 recognized her in this way: "In Appreciation to Edna Shoffner for the Years of Knowledge, Support and Strength You Have Given Us." In 1995, Edna retired as Practical Nursing Coordinator at the Tennessee Area Vocational Technical School in Shelbyville. At that time, she was honored by the staff and many of her former students with a plaque which included this tribute: "No one has done more for health care in Bedford County than she has."

Edna has been honored by members of the family: One grandchild wrote in her own words: "My role model's name is Edna Shoffner. I chose her as my role model because she has helped others all her life. She is very kind and very seldom ever gets mad or upset. She also teaches her seven grandchildren patience and kindness. She leads a special life by going to church and doing good deeds for others. Her students and her grandchildren still look up to her because she displays all the qualities of a special role model."

When our first born granddaughter was visiting her paternal GrandMother, she was asked if she would be jealous when the next grandchild was born in GrandMother Shoffner's family. She replied that she would not be jealous because GrandMother Shoffner would have plenty of love for all grandchildren.

Over the years, Edna and I have exchanged many expressions of affection. These have included little love notes, sometimes even an original poem, along with our gifts on birthdays, anniversaries, Christmas, and other special occasions. One such special occasion was our forty-fifth wedding anniversary on December 20, 1998. She became my "Lady of the Bracelet" when I presented her with a diamond bracelet containing forty-five diamonds, with the following message inscribed on the walnut jewelry box:

"To Edna, With Love For 45 years of your love

   December 20, 1953 - December 20, 1998."

In 1999, I painted her portrait in oil on canvas which I presented to her on Christmas eve, with this title: "Portrait of an Angel."

On September 22, 2001, I presented her with a copy of my book, in which I had written this entry:

"Edna, Dear, I would like for you to have this first book, of the last edition, with love for your patience and support, during the four years I worked on it. Allen."

I have looked back and read again that vow that I made nearly fifty years ago. I have honored her by being faithful to her, forsaking all others. I still love her. I still try to comfort her. My faith has been sorely tested, but with God's help, I will help her through her sickness.

Dec. 24, 1973

Dear Edna:

Here is a token of love for this Christmas. Please take this and select something you like, something personal and unique for you, such as a ring, furs, and something that you would never otherwise buy.

Remember, there will be no refunds or exchanges on this!

Love always,

Handwritten script dated
December 24, 1973

From Santa,
You don't know what to expect,
But with this you can select,
A piece of velvet, fur, or lace,
That will fit at the right place.
Love,

Allen

Another Christmas

Watercolor by Allen Shoffner
2006

A Poinsettia For Our
Loved One

Our Beloved Nurse

*Our Loved One and Our Three
Children, About 1967
Esther, Michael Allen, Melanie*

Some of the May Ways Our Loved One Loved All of
Our Grandchildren with Equal Love

Some of the May Ways Our Loved One Loved All of
Our Grandchildren with Equal Love

Some of the Many Ways Our Loved One Loved All of Our Grandchildren with Equal Love

Some of the Many Ways Our Loved One Loved All of Our Grandchildren with Equal Love

Our Loved One and Our Seven Grandchildren, 1991
Brannon, Reuben, Callie, Ryan, Sarah, Lauren, Elizabeth

My Loved One
September 20, 1992

THE FADING LIGHT

We started our journey through the valley of the shadow of darkness on June 23, 1998 in the office of a neurologist in Nashville, Tennessee. For the next five years this seemed more like a walk through the valley of the shadow of hell.

I realize that many others have walked through the valley of the shadow of darkness and death, suffering pain, disease, injury, and sickness. I have no reason to believe that our pain has been any greater or any different from others who have suffered similar sickness and pain. But I will write about ours, hoping that what I write may help others endure theirs and may help me and perhaps others be a better caregiver.

Edna began to have "short term memory loss" in 1998. The family noticed this but we did not think it was significant. Everybody forgets sometimes. She may have thought it was significant because she stopped driving. I noticed that she was having trouble with orientation. She was having difficulty in learning the switches on the range top. She even drew and posted on the refrigerator a diagram showing the arrangement and which surfaces the switches controlled. Dr. Charles Stimpson, our family physician, referred us to the neurologist for consultation. I knew that a neurologist was a medical doctor, specializing in the diagnosis and treatment of the diseases of the nervous system. The neurologist asked her questions to test orientation and recall, count backwards, spell backwards, and draw pictures. As I sat with her during the examination, I was not sure that I could draw any better pictures which seemed more like a game than a neurological examination. She had experienced and recovered from other medical serious problems, including the surgical replacement of an aortic valve, and we believed that her short term memory loss would itself be short term. Our belief was shaken when we received the doctor's report, containing his notes and clinical findings, including the CT scan. The report of his Mini-Mental State Exam was captioned: "A Treatment IND Program for Patients with Alzheimer's Disease."   He prescribed Aricept, which I later learned was for treatment of the disease. The neurologist reported that "her Mini mental status score was 23 out of 30 suggesting some significant cognitive impairment, likely reflecting a mild early degenerative dementia." How could this be? I tried to sort through and interpret the medical terminology. The doctor reported that there was no wandering, hallucinations, or seizures, no history of stroke, seizure, or serious neurological problems and no family history of dementia. How could such a diagnosis be made on the basis of the limited testing made by the neurologist? Could there be other reasons for the symptoms? My limited knowledge of Alzheimer's indicated that such a diagnosis could be made only by autopsy. Would it not be more logical to talk about symptoms of Alzheimer's rather than a diagnosis of Alzheimer's. I had talked to support groups about elder law, estate planning, and end of life issues, but I did not want to believe that this could be happening to the loved one in our family. I was in the first stage of "denial."

My legal training and experience made me somewhat skeptical. I wanted more proof. So, I tried to do some independent research. I read and clipped out news articles about Alzheimer's Disease. I read the statistics that this disease occurs in approximately ten percent of persons over age sixty-five. I was an optimist and believed that the remaining ninety per cent offered reasonable odds. I read the statistics that when doctors diagnose Alzheimer's Disease, the diagnosis is accurate eighty to ninety per cent of the time. I still remained an optimist and hoped that we would be included in the other twenty per cent. I read about the brain. I read about neurons and the "tangles and plaques" within the brain. But how, even with modern medical technology, can we know what is really happening within the complexities of the brain and mind? I read that this disease is no respecter of persons or gender, and that it destroys the minds of brilliant people, artists, and writers. I remembered that Nancy Reagan told Ronald Reagan the "long good-bye." Victims were referred to as "loved ones." I read that there is no cure and that the prescribed Aricept might only slow the course of the disease. I read about the symptoms which became more noticeable each day over a long period of time. With cancer and other deadly diseases, there is always hope for a cure and for life. With Alzheimer's Disease, there is no cure and no hope. I read in a leaflet distributed by the Alzheimer's Association that Alzheimer's is "The Disease of the Century" and "until a cure is found, death is inevitable."

I was not prepared mentally, physically, or spiritually, to accept this diagnosis and a death sentence for our loved one. But I did try to face the brutal reality and prepare myself as a caregiver. I read The 36 HOUR DAY (Mace & Rabins, Warner Books), the Mayo Clinic publication on Alzheimer's Disease (Peterson). I read in the literature distributed by the Alzheimer's Association the Ten Warning Signs of Caregiver Stress: Denial, Anger, Social Withdrawal, Anxiety, Depression, Exhaustion, Sleeplessness, Irritability, Lack of Concentration, and Health Problems. I did not then realize that I would personally experience all of these in watching an angel slowly die. I accepted the responsibility to comfort and keep in sickness the loved one who meant so much to me, as I had promised in our marriage vow.

Edna's memory loss became more noticeable and her orientation and mobility became progressively worse. So, we decided in February, 2002, while I was still in active law practice, that she would go to the "daybreak" program at the Shelbyville Assisted Living Center, where I left her in the mornings and picked her up in the afternoons. This continued for about a year, which allowed me to continue some limited law practice. While at assisted living, Edna seemed to be more functional for awhile, with less rigidity, more rational, without delusions, all of which I attributed to her activities at the center. She continued to be interested in helping residents there, many of whom were more disabled than she at that time. She talked to them about their problems. She wanted to be a "nurse" again.

March 26, 2002, was another day at Dr. Stimpson's office for a regular protime check for coumadin, which regulates the blood flow through the aortic valve. The doctor asked Edna to walk in the office, noticing the forward tilt, tested her reflexes, watched the noticeable tremor in her fingers, and told us what we had already feared: Parkinson's Disease. Another layer of sickness was added for which there was no cure.

In the early stages, Edna was aware of her memory loss. When I finished reading the Mayo Clinic publication on Alzheimer's Disease, I handed it to her, thinking that it was helpful to be informed. She read part of it, and we talked about it. I believe that she was aware of what we were facing, and I realized how horrible and frightening it must be for any person who is aware that all of her memory might fade into total darkness.

I tried to reassure her by talking with her and helping her fill in the "blank" spaces. Her memory loss was most noticeable in repeating questions and not remembering the day of the week and the time of day. She had problems in remembering what she wanted to say in conversations and in finding the right words. She was able to recognize friends but might not remember the names.

She continued to be disoriented. I did not leave her alone in the home, and even within the home I tried to stay within her "reach." Naturally, she relied upon me as her primary caregiver. She tended to "cling," and wanted me "to hold" her and be in her presence as much as possible. One night I heard a frightening sound and saw her lying prone on her back at the door to the bathroom. I jumped up and cradled her in my arms, thinking that she might be dead. We slept in adjoining single beds, which we pulled together to prevent her from falling on the floor on one side and used a bed rail on the other side.   Occasionally, she awoke from what seemed to be a bad dream. On one occasion, she awoke with tremors which seemed like a seizure. When this happened, I comforted her by hugging her tightly and she relaxed. I awoke many nights listening, wondering if she was still breathing. When awake she was usually rational and maintained a good attitude. But she was fearful and sometimes even when awake, she said she saw things or persons which I did not see.

Edna continued to lose mobility. She could walk in the early stages, but she fell several times, sometimes with injury, and I usually led her by holding her hand, especially up and down steps and in unfamiliar locations. I "tucked" her into bed at night, and led her to the bathroom when she had to use it at night, which was usually two or three times each night. Her vision was impaired and she was not able to write legibly. I gave her a phone with extra large dial buttons and a reading lamp. Esther prepared and hung on the wall a large board on which she wrote familiar phone numbers in large letters and numbers.

Edna needed help dressing and undressing. I helped her dress in the mornings and dress for bed at night. In helping her dress and undress I noticed considerable stiffness in her arms and legs. She always wanted to be dressed appropriately, but when she tried to do this herself, she usually reversed the clothes (back to front and also inside out), and sometimes "layered" the clothes. She needed help in buttoning garments and tying shoes.

She was able to do some personal care for a time, such as brushing her teeth, but she did not have the dexterity to floss her teeth which I did for her. She was unable do her own baths or showers which our daughter, Esther, and I did for her. She usually needed help in using the bathroom. She wore "briefs" and she was unable to change these herself. She appeared to be losing control of normal bodily functions, which apparently she was not even aware of. Edna has always been a very refined person, and this problem would have been very embarrassing to her.

I cooked and prepared our meals. I tried to prepare nutritious meals which fit Edna's needs, and for a time she was able to eat without significant assistance, except, for example, cutting meats.

I helped monitor her medications, but occasionally after a bad day both of us missed the evening medication.

I did most of the household cleaning that was done, but Edna tried to do some light chores around the house, which I encouraged to help her feel needed and independent. She tired easily and took frequent long naps during the day.

The night of March 23, 2002, was a very emotional time for both of us. Edna called me about 3 a.m., when she was awakened by tremors, jerking of arms, legs, and other muscles. She wanted me to sleep with her. She was fearful, and I slept close to her until sunrise. I realized how our life together was changing and in some ways had been reversed. I had visions of Edna changing diapers, tucking the children in bed, comforting them, soothing their fears, and saying good night prayers with them; and now I was tucking her in bed, changing her pads, and saying my prayers for her in the silence and privacy of the night. I thought of the way in which nature seemed to compensate for injury or loss: That when one arm, hand, foot, eye, or ear is taken away, the other tends to compensate. I felt that this natural law also applied to spouses who had promised to keep each other in sickness as well as in health.

As I lay beside Edna that night waiting for the sunrise, I made the decision which I had tried to delay as long as I could: That I would suspend or close my law practice.

The days turned into weeks, the weeks into months, and months into years, and all seemed to merge together.

July 24, 2002, was one of the most emotional days in my life. I had earlier made the decision to close my law practice I realized that I was not able to focus effectively on law practice and that I was making some minor, but embarrassing, mistakes. I started preparing my last newsletter for my clients, announcing that I would be suspending my practice effective October 1, 2002. I placed my law license in inactive status, canceled legal publications, closed my law books, and hung up my briefcase. I had practiced my chosen profession for nearly fifty years and I had been married to my loved one for nearly fifty years, and now I realized that I was losing both.

I continued to take Edna to assisted living while I wound up pending legal matters. I tried to continue as primary caregiver. She continued to decline. On more than one occasion at church, when I was an usher, she became disoriented and did not know how to return to her seat without my help. I privately choked away my tears.

On October 31, 2002, I went by Dr. Stimpson's office to discuss another prescription which was supposed to make the Parkinson's medicine more effective. He told me what I already had first denied and later accepted: that Edna would not get any better. He also told me that I would probably not be physically able to continue indefinitely as caretaker.

I soon found that Dr. Stimpson was right. I had done heavy physical labor on the farm; I did not smoke or drink hard liquor; I had maintained good health habits; and I thought I was pretty tough and physically fit. I had continued regular exercise on home exercise equipment, thinking that by staying physically fit I would be better able to help Edna.

On November 1, 2002, I awoke at 2:15 a.m. and lay awake until the morning light came in the windows. I realized that anger and bitterness was festering within me. That morning I did not say the usual grace with Edna at breakfast. I was losing faith. What was there to be thankful for?

Edna said grace alone. Her faith remained strong; mine was diminished.

Edna was on life's edge again that November. She was taken to the emergency room when she lost blood caused by diverticulitis, requiring four bags of blood and a week in the critical care unit.

November 30, 2002, another Saturday, was our usual day to get her hair done and go to the grocery. But this Saturday was different. Her expression was different. There was no spark or life in her eyes. I was supposed to be tough and able to handle emotions, but when I found a private place I cried again. I knew that she was dying a slow death.

The light of Edna's mind continued to fade, but she retained her natural warmth and deep faith.

We were unable to continue daybreak at assisted living. When I picked her up one day, I realized that she would soon need a higher level of care. I could tell that she had had a bad day. Her facial expression was not normal, and she seemed to be drifting away in a fog. I spent another restless night and started another restless day. Edna and I had cried together and we had prayed together many times. I continued to lose faith and hope. I wanted to cry again, but I had run out of tears. I wanted to pray but I had run out of prayers.

When we left assisted living, we had to make some adjustments in caregiving. I spent more time at home. We were fortunate to have two children living close to home. Our son, Michael Allen, was always ready to help. His wife, Gay, also a Registered Nurse, had been with Edna during critical illnesses. Our daughter, Esther, a Registered Physical Therapist, always knew exactly how to make her Mother more comfortable and helped consistently with her personal care. Esther's husband, Tim, was a dutiful son-in-law, always available for support. Occasionally the grandchildren would help. And, of course, the children also had, at the same time, responsibilities to their own families and work to consider. We were also fortunate to have a saintly elderly friend, partially handicapped herself, who had done some domestic work for us over the years and agreed to help when she was able. Reba Buchanan, a deeply religious person, has a place waiting for her in Heaven.

We were thankful for the good days. On April 11, 2003, we dined out together for the first time in a long time, which for me was a welcome diversion from the kitchen. We ate at Red Lobster where we usually liked to eat. Our favorite waitress there always liked to tell us about her child. This young lady sensed that Edna was not the same person she had served many times before and that she needed help handling her food. She hugged both of us as we left. That was the last time we ate there.

We were thankful for a good day on Easter Sunday, April 20, 2003. Our family attended church services together and then adjourned to Cortner Mill near Normandy for buffet lunch, where I saw and talked to old friends I had not seen in awhile.

On good days I encouraged her to exercise by walking with me to the mail box. These rare good days passed quickly and then every day became a struggle. I would get up in the early morning, thinking that the day would be better than the last one. I would fix our breakfast, help Edna up out of bed and to the bathroom, help her dress, and give her the medicine, then we would slide down hill the rest of the day. After I prepared our dinner, cleaned up the dishes, helped Edna to dress for bed, we were both exhausted. I began to say and do things that left me feeling guilty and we ended the day worse than the one before.

Edna fell many times, fortunately without serious injury, and we were concerned that next time she might fall and break her hip. The family had discussed care options from time to time, including home care. Another was a nursing home. I investigated the Homewood Residence, a facility in Nashville specializing in the care of Alzheimer's patients. We agreed that distance would limit our visitation there. We investigated the nursing homes in Shelbyville. I knew that for many a nursing home was a stop on the way to a funeral home. This was part of the agony of saying "good-bye." That night, as I looked to her across the bed, I asked myself: How does one prepare for the empty bed after sleeping beside each other for more than fifty years? I cried myself to sleep.

Edna had bad dreams at night. She also had visions during the day. When talking to me, she would refer to me as "he" or "Allen." She referred to herself as "she" as if she were a third person. She would look out the window and see our son, Michael Allen, on his green John Deere tractor. I would look but did not see him. She believed that other people were in the house, which she referred to sometimes as "phantoms," including one who helped me around the house. Sometimes, she talked about the "little children," who sat at the dinner table waiting to be fed. She talked very rationally about these persons who did not have names, but who were very real to her. I did not disagree but simply nodded my head as if they did exist.

There was one vision that pulled on my heart. One day I noticed that she was in Michael Allen's room, largely left intact years ago when he left for school. Edna was not aware that I was watching her. She was placing and arranging pillows on the bed. When she finished, I walked into the room and asked her what she had been doing. She said that she was placing the pillows to keep "the little girl" who was sleeping there from falling off the bed. Upon reflection, I began to think that these visions could be real. I had been waiting for a voice from the heavens or a burst of light from the sky which had not come to me. But many people of faith have experienced visions and miracles. Mortals may not "see" what may be present. I know that Edna is a person with deep religious faith. Does everything in our mortal life have to be seen, touched, heard, scientifically or mathematically proven, certified, and stamped with a seal before being accepted as truth?

Edna and I had talked occasionally about nursing home care. She had even placed both of our names on the "waiting list" at one of the nursing homes years ago. A "waiting list" did not then sound threatening, and we wanted to wait as long as possible. I knew that it would be difficult to face the reality of going to a nursing home now and it would be difficult for us to even talk about it. One morning she told me of a dream she had during the night: She said that she went with me to Nashville to look at the

Homewood Residence, and that she came back home, leaving me sitting there alone. I told her that this was a fitting way to end the dream.

Watercolor by Allen Shoffner
2006

Wild Daisies for Our
Loved One

TESTS OF FAITH

The turbulent days and restless nights continued. I resented having to close my law practice. I missed the clients and friends that I had known over the years. The resentment, anger, and bitterness which had been festering within me was consuming my mind and body. My blood pressure trended up. I did not take medication for insomnia or depression. I did not ask for help. I felt that I was falling into a black pit which had no bottom. I was breaking apart physically and emotionally. I was losing control. Edna and I went to bed tired and disturbed, sometimes not even telling each other goodnight as we had always done. I found myself being impatient and ill with her. Sometimes I said cruel things to her. I asked myself: How can I feel this way toward one that I have loved for fifty years? I realized that Edna had no control over what was happening to her, and I was beginning to have no control as her caregiver. I felt the crushing mental pain of guilt, asked for forgiveness, and resolved to try to be a better caregiver the next day.

I also lost part of my spirit. I lost interest in doing the things which I enjoyed doing. I could not focus. I just did not care any more. Except for family members and a few neighbors, nobody else seemed to care either. We found ourselves isolated and withdrawing from social relationships. I noticed that with a few exceptions our friends were not calling or visiting. Some may have been concerned, but they did not let us know it. Maybe they did not feel comfortable facing our grim reality. My perception that nobody seemed to care fueled my anger and bitterness. I realized later that this perception was not justified and that I was just too proud to ask for help. I wanted to protect our privacy. I thought that I had a super human ability to handle caregiving and could do it all by myself. I realize now that this attitude was a mistake.

If anything can be learned from this experience, it is this: Get help, even if it has to be begged for, because it may not be offered, and don't wait too long to get it.

I had tried to prepare our family for sickness and death. We both had Living Wills, Durable Powers of Attorney, Durable Powers of Attorney for Health Care, Testamentary Wills, and even Family Living Trusts. But there was no effective way to prepare adequately for the financial "spend down" caused by long term care.

But the worse loss of all was my loss of spiritual faith. I cursed the darkness. I cursed the demons. I cursed for the least excuse, and most of the time for no excuse at all. I have never heard Edna say a bad word of any kind about anything or anybody, and I know that my anger distressed her which made me feel guilty again. I stopped saying mealtime grace with Edna. I stopped praying. I lost belief in things I had been taught in childhood. Why didn't God cast out the demons? Where was God? I searched for answers to this question and for my lack of faith.

THE NURSING HOME

In August, 2003, I made an appointment with the Administrator of the Glen Oaks Convalescent Center in Shelbyville for a walk-through. Glen Oaks provided skilled care and convalescence for patients discharged from hospitals, but it was also licensed as a nursing home. I did not want to keep anything from Edna, so I asked her to go with me. She was pleased to see several nurses there who had been her students. Years ago, my Mother had been a patient in the same facility, but no one can ever really feel at home in a nursing home. Even a walk-through is depressing. I noticed several ladies clutching dolls, trying to hang on to their memories of their children and motherhood. Several residents lay in contorted shapes in beds, with twisted faces, mouths open. Some looked more dead than alive, already in the next world, and I was reminded of the narrow boundary between life and death. Some who seemed awake sat in wheel chairs in the halls and around the nurses' stations, with the blank expressions, perhaps hoping that someone, even a stranger, would stop and talk to them. This was not what I had envisioned for the rest of our lives.

On August 20, 2003, Edna's name was placed on the waiting list at Glen Oaks. August 29, 2003, was one of the saddest days in my life. This was the day on which Dr. Stimpson made arrangements for the nursing home. He first sent "orders" for Edna's admission to the hospital the next day as the first step in the transition. Bless her heart. She wanted to help me pack for the trip. She even took out my pajamas from the drawers and my toothbrush from the bathroom. I had to tell her that I would not be going. I wished that I could take her place.

The Administrator, Assistant Administrator, and the staff were very professional in making our transition to the nursing home as painless as possible. The nurses and attendants working there have a hard job to do, and most work hard under hard circumstances. I realized that facilities such as Glen Oaks perform a needed service in the long term care of persons who can no longer be effectively cared for by families or caregivers.

GRIEF AND LONELINESS

August 30th was another long day. After I came home from the hospital that night, I could not bring myself to lie down next to the empty bed. I went back to the hospital twice that night before coming back home and finally trying to sleep.

On September 2nd, we made the transition to the skilled care section of the nursing home. There was a hint of fall in the air on September 4th, which made me more sad and lonely.

On September 6th, Edna was readmitted to the hospital for treatment of a urinary tract infection, discharged on September 10th, and returned the same day to the nursing home.

One night when Edna was in the nursing home and I was at home alone, I heard her calling me, "Allen!" just as she had called me during the nights many times before. I jumped from a light sleep, even answering her aloud, and then I realized that my loved one was not in the bed next to me but in the nursing home. I had awakened from a bad dream.

The family started the routine visits to the nursing home. I usually fed Edna lunch, and Michael and Esther usually rotated to feed her the evening meal. But the long, lonely days and nights continued at home.

September 27th was such a day. I was at home alone, looking out the window at the fall rain. I was so lonely. My loved one had devoted her life to taking care of other people, and now she was dying a slow death at Glen Oaks nursing home. Why was her intellect taken and mine spared? Why could this not have happened to me? Life was not fair. I was still unable to find faith in life again.

My spirit was lifted that afternoon at the graduation ceremony of the 2003 Practical Nursing Program at the Tennessee Technology Center when the Edna Shoffner Award for Honor and Excellence was awarded to an outstanding graduate. This was also an honor for Edna, who was unable to attend the ceremony, and I was honored to have a part in establishing and funding this annual award.

Edna had always remembered the birthdays of the children and grandchildren and prepared birthday cards for them. I started doing these after she was not able. She tried to add her name to the last ones but she could only touch the pen and scratch a mark. As I looked back at the calendar, I saw where she had some time earlier made a note in her weak handwriting, hardly legible, "Edna's Birthday" for an October 7th entry, and entered in the same way the word: "Anniversary" on another October date. I realized later that the reference to our anniversary was probably the last time that she had tried to write. I hoped that she would remember, when we reached our fiftieth anniversary on December 20, 2003.

On September 30th, after I had fed Edna she whispered in her soft voice: "Take me home with you." These words continue to haunt me.

Our struggles continued in the nursing home. Edna was released from skilled care on Monday, October 10th, and transferred to the intermediate care section in a private room, which we tried to make as much like home as possible with pictures, furniture, television and items that she might recognize. Monitoring her medication continued in an effort to reach the precise level for Parkinson's Disease. She continued to decline in mobility. I helped take her down to the hairdresser. It is difficult to describe in my words the rigidity in her arms, neck, and legs, which seemed like the rigors of death itself. She could not feed herself, so we began feeding her, mostly with a spoon a small bite at a time.

On another day in October, after I had returned from feeding Edna lunch at the nursing home, I dropped into another deep depression, as I watched the leaves falling from the maple trees in the brisk fall wind. I thought about how rigid Edna was at lunch that day when I tried to feed her. She gripped her hands into fists and wrapped her arms across her chest, refusing to release when I tried to force movement. We determined then that we must help her regain some mobility and get her to walking again, or risk spending the rest of her life in a wheel chair or confined to a bed. Susan McCurry, the director of nurses, helped set up a program of restoration therapy. In addition to therapy by the attendants, we started a routine of assisting her to walk in the hall.

Another type of therapy helped both of us. Occasionally, I would whisper in her ear: "I love you," and she would respond and whisper to me: "I love you too," as she had done many times before.

One day in November, as I drove down the driveway to feed Edna lunch at the nursing home, I noticed a single white rose blooming on the rose bush which I had planted years ago along the driveway. This was truly the "last rose of summer," which had bloomed during a few warm days of fall. I stopped, cut the rose from the thorns, put it in a vase, and took it to Edna.

Our children continued to be supportive. Esther is much like Edna, compassionate and caring, spending most of her time helping others, along with her own family, never complaining. Michael Allen is always available, very kind and attentive to Edna, feeding her, sharing in the caregiving, never complaining, Melanie is not able to share actively in care because of distance, but she would if she were here.

I continued to be lonely and grieve, awaking at night and remaining awake two or three hours. During this period of time, in an effort to relieve my depression and grief, I did some portraiture and scenes in oil on canvas, and even tried writing some poetry. One was a desolate winter scene of a lone dead oak tree under cloudy skies, which reflected my desolation, despair, and depression. I titled this painting: "The Old Man," and wrote this poem:

The Old Man just stands now,
Facing the winter storm alone
Weathered and worn by winter winds
From a hundred winters gone
With snow upon the brow
And limbs broken and bare
He will fall away and decay,
And return to the Earth from which he grew
But from acorns dropped he will live anew.

FINDING FAITH

I tried to restore my faith by reading the Bible. I had read parts of the Bible, but I had never read it from cover to cover. So during periods of despair, anger, and bitterness, I read the Bible. I read the New Century Version Bible given to me by a friend, starting in Genesis and finishing in Revelation. The Book of Job offered some comfort, but I did not find what I was looking for in the Old Testament. Maybe God did not owe us mercy, but I still had the question: Why did a merciful God allow bad things happen to good people?

I began to find the answer to faith in Corinthians, where Paul writes: "So we do not give up. Our physical body is becoming older and weaker, but our spirit inside us is made new every day. We have small troubles for a while now, but they are helping us gain an eternal glory that is much greater than the troubles. We set our eyes not on what we see but on what we cannot see. What we see will last only a short time, but what we cannot see will last forever." 2 Corinthians, 4, 16.

I also found answers in Edna's faith. She has taught me faith. She has restored my faith. I believe that angels exist. They may not appear to us on wings or with halos, but they are around us when we are not aware. I truly believe that Edna is an angel. I found God through her. She made me a better person. Things which I had thought important and strived for were no longer important. I have learned again the power and peace of prayer.

I also found faith from things in the world around me that can be seen. I have seen the flowers and lowly plants searching for the light, their heads leaning away from the darkness toward the sunlight. Why were these plants drawn to the light? It was God's way, Nature's way, a small part of creation, that even plants are endowed with capacity to reach for the light to sustain life. I have seen the tulips flourish in full bloom in the Spring, die and wilt away, and then come again in another Spring.

Today, while writing, I looked out the door and noticed a squirrel in the yard. I had never really stopped very long to watch the squirrels and birds in the yard. But I believe that we can learn and gain spiritual strength from observing nature around us. This squirrel, carrying a walnut in its mouth, scurried nervously around the yard, stopping occasionally and standing erectly to be sure that no predator was watching. After cautiously and deliberately checking out several locations, the squirrel found a place where he thought he could safely bury the nut. Nature has provided this squirrel with the simple natural instinct to know later exactly where that nut is buried and he will return later in the winter to claim it. Nature is full of examples of the ways in which God has provided for all creation, even the smallest creatures and the blades of grass under our feet: The instinct of homing pigeons to return home, the instinct of salmon to return to their spawning waters, and other species of God's creation which struggle to return and die at the place of their creation. Miracles are happening around us all of the time without our even knowing it.

Paul uses a very simple example in 1 Corinthians, 15, 36, to illustrate how we will be raised from the dead: A seed when planted in the ground "must die in the ground before it can live and grow."

Even though the bloom fades and the petals fall and die, life returns from the ground and life really never dies. Our spirit and soul rests within us like a seed waiting to bloom again.

One day when I was filled with despair, loneliness, and guilt, I sat down and wrote this love letter to my Loved One, struggling to find the right words:.

> To My Angel:
> O, my Darling, I miss you so much,
> I sit here at home alone,
> You have been taken away,
> I think about you night and day,
> I lost you years ago,
> But I will find you again another day,
> I miss your sweet smile,
> I miss your soft voice,
> I miss leading you by the hand each step of the way,
> I miss holding you tight,
> I miss all the other things we used to share,
> I miss your love, the Light of my Life.
>
> Forgive me when I was unkind,
> Forgive me when I was impatient,
> Forgive me when I lost my faith,
> Forgive me for not telling you every day:
>   "I love you."
>
> I thank you for your love,
> I thank you for teaching me patience,
> I thank you for your kindness, and above all,
> I thank you for leading me back to faith.
>
> Love Always, Allen.

My loved one was not able to read this love letter. She will not be able to read this love story, but she will understand when I present it to her on our Golden Wedding Anniversary.

No one has expressed love in the English language better than Elizabeth Barrett Browning:

How do I love thee? Let me count the ways.
I love thee to the depth, breadth and height
My soul can reach, when feeling out of sight
For the ends of Being and ideal Grace.
I love thee to the level of everyday's
Most quiet need, by sun and candlelight.
I love thee freely, as men strive for Right,
I love thee purely, as they turn from Praise.
I love thee with a passion put to use
In my old griefs, and with my childhood's faith.
I love thee with a love I seemed to lose
With my lost saints-I love thee with the breath,
Smiles, tears, all of my life!-and, if God choose,
I shall but love thee better after death.

OUR LIFE, DAY BY DAY

I had taken a leave of absence from law practice and closed my office in October, 2002, to be a caretaker for Edna. During this period of time, the routine for her care continued day to day until the decision was made to enter Glen Oaks in August, 2003. During this leave of absence at home with Edna, I renewed my childhood interest in art and painting in both oils and watercolor. I completed several portraits and scenes in oil. This activity absorbed some of my restlessness and depression. Finally, I reopened my law office in June, 2004. I could not expect my old clients to wait eighteen months for me. I lost some, but some returned, and I found new ones. I felt blessed that I was able to return to active practice.

But the priority of my life remained my Loved One. My love story continues day to day. I hope that it never ends, but I know that it will some day.

On September 1, 2004, we started another year in the nursing home. I had not missed a day feeding her at least once a day, sometimes twice, for the past three hundred sixty-five consecutive days. I considered this a privilege, not a chore. It was a part of my life. The children continued to feed her the evening meal every day.

Prayer is also now part of my life. I have prayed for Edna every day. I have the faith that my prayers are heard, but I still have trouble understanding why God allows some life to be so unfair. Then, I understand that our standard of fairness may not be God's measure. So, it is better to pray that God's will be done, not mine or ours.

On Sunday, September 5th, I asked our pastor at church about communion for Edna. A few days later, when I went to the nursing home to feed her, I noticed a note he had left on the table, along with two communion cups and wafers. He had written on the note: "Communion- consecrated for two. Please celebrate with Edna. God Bless you both."

I had received communion many times before, but I had never given communion. I do not feel worthy of receiving communion, and I certainly did not feel worthy of giving the Holy Sacraments to Edna. When I asked her if she wanted to share communion, her expression indicated a positive response. I did not have at the nursing home the Common Book of Worship containing the words for the administration of communion. I had repeated the words many times in a routine way, like many worshipers in the church service, without thinking of what these words really meant to me. But I used in a stumbling way the unscripted and unrehearsed words which I believed were meant for me to use for this special occasion. Sharing this communion with Edna was an emotional experience for me and I believe a meaningful one for Edna.

Later, at home, I read and reflected upon the words of the Holy Sacrament, including the Nicene Creed:
"I believe in one God, the Father Almighty, maker of heaven and
earth, And, of all things visible and invisible

****

And I look for the Resurrection of the dead; And the Life of the world to come. Amen."

A few days later, the pastor told me that he had not given the sacraments to her because she did not seem "aware" that the sacraments were being offered. Does this mean that Holy Communion has no spiritual value or meaning for a person with dementia?

I believed that God was answering my prayers when I went to the nursing home on September 15th. I told her as I had done on every day before that I loved her. She said: "I love you too."

September 17, 2004 was a rewarding day for the family. That was the occasion for the award to the second recipient of the Edna Shoffner Award of Honor and Excellence at the graduation ceremony of the practical nursing program at the Tennessee Technology Center.

October 7th was Edna's birthday. I brought a bouquet of flowers with me when I went in to feed her, but she was not responsive. She appeared to be in a trance and did not even open her eyes. I finally abandoned the effort to arouse her and left the flowers on the table. I returned to the nursing home that evening to feed her. As I was leaving she held my hand tightly, telling me in a silent way that she did not want me to go. She asked: "What did Mother say?" This had meaning to her, but not to me. I left there again with a sad feeling about her. My spirit was lifted some that evening watching our granddaughter, Callie, play in the soccer tournament in Winchester.

Thanksgiving Day, 2004: The family brought Edna "home" for the day.

January 13, 2005: This was the 500th consecutive day I had fed Edna lunch. The pastor had visited her earlier, but she was not aware for communion, and he left the sacraments again for me, which we shared together.

January 20, 2005: Today was different and special. As I was leaving after lunch, I hugged her again and as we looked into each other's eyes, I told her: "I love you," and she said: "I love you too." I moved closer and kissed her lightly on the lips.

But a few days later, Sunday, February 6, 2005, when I went in to feed Edna, our world changed again. The lifeless expression, the veil over her eyes had returned, and my despondency returned. She struggled to swallow the small bites which I spooned to her lips.

Other days came and passed, most depressing my spirit, a few lifting it.

April 9, 2005: As I sat at home alone today looking out the window, I thanked God for the beautiful tulips in bloom again this year. The hollies and blue berry bushes were in full bloom, filling the spring air with the sweet smell of nectar, which the bees were gathering in exchange for pollinating the little flowers.

As I sat down to eat that day, I thought of the beautiful childhood grace thanking God for his Blessings:
"God is good,
 God is great,
 Let us thank him for our food."

April 10, 2005: The first barn swallows arrived today, guarding the same nest they built and from which they hatched young last year. How did they remember to return to the same nest? How can anyone doubt that there is an intelligent design of our world made by its Creator?

Watercolor by Allen Shoffner
2006

An Easter Lily for Our
Loved One

UNDER THE CROSS

Saturday, June 11, 2005: I sit here at home alone another day. But my loneliness and spirit is lifted some as I look out the kitchen window. I had placed there close to the window a small clay flower vase. I do not know the name of the plant, but it was one which Edna had started in the vase and which I had cared for following her sickness. When she was in assisted living, a child had made and given to her a simple wooden cross made by crossing two sticks of wood bound together by yarn. This cross had been placed in the vase above the plant. During the winters I had cared for the arrangement inside, which I   moved outside in the spring to a protected place under the window. This spring a Mother Wren had built her nest in a protected place amid the leaves of the plant. This nest was immediately below the arms of the cross. I peeped today into the carefully prepared and protected nest. Five eggs were awaiting God's call to life.

This simple rustic cross had become more than a symbol to me. I look toward it and gain spiritual strength each morning as I say my breakfast prayers, thanking God for His Great Creation and everything in it, our food, the many other blessings of life, and especially for sharing his Angel, Edna, with me, and praying for her recovery. The Mother Wren and the way in which she had built her nest and protected her eggs, were also meaningful to me. The nest reminded me of how Edna had built her nest, protected, and cared for our family in the place where I am now living alone. The Cross reminded me that God, like the Mother who never abandons her nest, never abandons those beneath the cross. Soon, we will all be born anew and fly away from our earthly nest like the little birds.

Watercolor by Allen Shoffner 2006

A Rose for Our Loved One

ANOTHER DAY, ANOTHER YEAR

This is September 1, 2005. My loved one has been away for two years today, seven hundred thirty long days and nights of loneliness. But I have thanked God for each of those days that he has shared his Angel with me. I thank God that He has helped me help her by feeding her lunch, bite by bite, each of those seven hundred thirty consecutive days. I believe that she looks for me each day and seems to hear me coming, walking down the long hall to her room. I whisper in her ear each day that I love her and she understands. I press my face to hers and embrace her tightly. Yet, some times she drifts away and seems to be in another strange place so far away. She is dying slowly from Parkinson's Disease, which is like death itself. She can not stand; she locks her arms across her chest; she can not move her legs. I continue to wake in the middle of the night, thinking about her, fearing the call which I know will come some day or some night. I am reminded again how unfair life is: I am able to move, get up, and continue many of life's normal activities, recognize and talk to people, while she sits every hour of every day in a wheel chair, recliner, or a nursing home bed. The hardest part of this for me to accept is that some of our friends have stopped visiting and calling. But I try to understand that they do not want to face the living remains of a person they once enjoyed seeing, a beautiful vibrant lady, who never complained, a totally unselfish person who spent her active life helping other people. She will always be the best part of my life. I thank God for Esther and Michael Allen who have been there with me for her, and for Melanie's calls, as we struggle each day to keep our Angel as long as we can on this side of Heaven. I pray each day that He will bring her back to health and life.

September 22, 2005: A depressing day. When I went in today to feed Edna, I had the sense that I was losing her. She looked at me in a strange way, as if she did not know who I was or why I was there. She swallowed with difficulty. I left with the feeling of helplessness and hopelessness.

September 24, 2005: A better day. This was the day for the graduation ceremony honoring the 2005 LPN graduates from the Tennessee Technology Center, which was held this year at the University of Tennessee Space Institute. This was the third year at which the Edna Shoffner Award of Honor and Excellence was awarded to the outstanding student. The award was presented by Ivan Jones, the TTC director, to Nicole Edinger. He referred to Edna as setting the "Gold Standard" for nurses. This was another impressive ceremony and very meaningful to me and our family.

October 7, 2005: Edna's birthday. When I went in today to feed her lunch, I was not sure that she even knew it was her birthday. How could any birthday like hers be a happy birthday? But I acted as if it were.

November 12, 2005: Tonight, Esther, Michael Allen, and I joined to stand Edna up on her feet. She has been completely immobile, sitting or lying twenty-four hours day and night. She tends to lean in the chair when sitting and can not even adjust herself in the chair. We believe holding her a few minutes while she stands helps her and it surely helps us to do something besides seeing her sit with her arms locked across her chest. She can still chew, but continues to have difficulty swallowing at times. I am fearful that she will choke.

When I see Edna "down," I am also down. I don't want her to die alone in the nursing home. I want to take her home with me.

December 20, 2005: Today was our fifty-second wedding anniversary. When I went in to feed her lunch, I said what I usually said: "Hi, Sweetheart," and loved her by kissing her in her ear. I did not know if she was aware it was our anniversary, and I did not mention it. After I left, I felt guilty and depressed that I did not observe it with flowers.

December 24, 2005: Another Christmas in the nursing home. The family gathered in Edna's room bringing gifts. Melanie and our granddaughter, Elizabeth, were here this year. But there was no joy. Edna was away in another world and was not even able to see the gifts which were opened for her.

New Year's Day, 2006: This was the first day I missed feeding Edna lunch because I had an old fashioned cold which I did not want to bring in to her. But I did go by the nursing home to let the staff know.

January 5, 2006: This was the day Edna was moved from Glen Oaks to Bedford County Nursing Home. The family had considered this move over a period of time, believing that it would be better for her to be at the other nursing home where Gay was Director of Nurses.

January 22, 2006: The sad and lonely days continue. The weather outside is dark, dreary, and depressing. I had been listening to classical music while I was writing this, and Mozart's Requiem started playing on the DVD. Even the music was sad and depressing. I did not realize, until I read about the great composer, that this melancholy music was written by Mozart as a ritual for the dead, when he himself was depressed and had a premonition about his own death, and that he died at the age of thirty-five before it was completed.

Our family sadly faced the ritual of Death this past week. Frances Pack, Gay's mother, died suddenly Sunday, January 15th. As I followed in the funeral procession to the cemetery behind the police escort, part of the ritual of death, I thought that sometimes some worthy persons, like Frances Pack, never get a police escort until after they die.

Edna continues to die a little each day. The wake for her continues each day in the nursing home. A small part of her is buried each day. When I go in each day to feed her, I greet her as if she were still the same person I married over fifty-two years ago. I say: "Sweetheart, what have you done today?" But she does not answer now. She does not speak. She does not open her eyes. I do not know if she even knows I am there. I feed her each bite. She struggles to chew and swallow.

Before I leave, I whisper in her ear that I love her. I touch her but I cannot reach her. Oh, how much I would like to know that she knows that I love her. She seems to be so far away, beyond a veil that separates us.

This love story is a tribute to my Loved One. But this love story would not be complete without a tribute to other loved ones in the family who have shared in her care and fight to keep her in life. Esther and Gay are like Edna in many ways, observant of patients, knowledgeable about treatment and medical procedures, and above all compassionate. Each of them has an instinctive ability to know where and why a patient hurts and what to do about it. I have noticed how Edna responds to Michael Allen when he is present and how he expresses his love when he feeds her and talks to her. I have seen our first born grandson, Ryan, who is challenged in some ways not experienced by other children, show his kindness and tenderness toward her. The other grandchildren show their kindness in different ways. I recognize that the stress of caring for a loved one increases the stress within a family, but Tim continues to support Esther in Edna's care, without any complaint or expression of impatience.

Our family has always been close. Of course, our children have experienced the normal sibling rivalries and even occasional disagreements with parents, which have usually been either forgiven or forgotten by the next day; and none of our children has ever been estranged from us, or estranged from each other, unlike the unfortunate experience of parents and siblings in many families. Esther has not only been a healer of broken bodies, but she has been a healer of broken spirits and hurt feelings as well.

Although we have been separated over the years by geography, Melanie and the family has remained close in other ways. I wrote her a personal letter a few days ago, enclosing some notes which she had written to me on November 24, 1962, when she was only eight years old. She had included her Santa Claus list, and she wanted to know if I was Santa Claus, and she wanted to be sure that I loved her. She had scribbled on school tablet paper: "Do you love me? Yes or No." "Will you kiss me? Yes or No." "Do you think I am sweet? Yes or No." I had kept these little treasured notes in my family "archives" for forty-three years and I assured her in my recent letter to her that yes, I still loved her as I did then.

Our fight to keep our loved one with us as long as we can has even brought our family closer.

I also want to give thanks and pay tribute to other persons around us who save lives, make us safer, more comfortable, and more secure. I admire and respect the people who don't mind getting their hands dirty doing dirty jobs and experiencing some of the unfairness in life, while sometimes others stand back watching, living off their labor.

They are found in hospitals and nursing homes, giving medications, watching monitors, changing pads, lifting, turning, bathing, and feeding patients, cleaning soiled beds, mopping floors and doing the exhausting labor required to maintain life.

They are found on the farm, working at high risk to personal safety, in hard labor producing what we eat, with little reward for that labor.

They are found in the classroom, where our teachers struggle to teach our children and grandchildren under adverse conditions for unfair compensation.

They are found in the mines, doing the dark, dirty, and dangerous work digging deep holes in the earth, from which they may, or may not, return.

They are found in the fire halls and police stations, exposed to personal risk in maintaining safety and security. They are found driving trucks carrying things which we depend on for every day life. They are found in the many other occupations required to keep life in this country going: Carpenters, brick layers, stone masons, plumbers, electricians, mechanics, engineers, craftsmen in many trades, and laborers who do the grunting and heavy lifting.

They include our best young men and women sent to kill or be killed while the military-industrial complex is enriched by the spoils of war.

Watercolor by Allen Shoffner.
2006

Morning Glories for
Our Loved One

A FIGHT FOR LIFE

On the evening of February 7, 2006, Esther and Gay noticed a sudden decline in Edna's vital signs, including a life threatening drop in blood pressure and what appeared to be seizures. She was taken to the emergency room, then admitted to the critical care unit of the hospital for several days where she received blood to replace internal bleeding, and various IV medications. Then, it was to the hospital once more, and back to the nursing home.

Valentine's Day, February 14, 2006: For several days before this year's Valentine's Day, I had been very fearful, even with a superstitious premonition, that Edna might die on Valentine's Day. Her Mother died on Valentine's Day in 1975. Death has been called a "horizon," beyond which we can not see. Edna was close to this horizon. There were no flowers, boxes of candy, or parties, on this Valentine's Day, but at the end of the day, we still had our Loved One.

February 26, 2006: I noticed today that the birds are returning to the yard. It is still winter according to my calendar and it still looks like winter out my window. Do the birds know something I don't, or are they just optimistic that spring will come soon?

March 2, 2006: Edna refused to eat today. She had not eaten well for the last several days, but today she even refused to open her mouth. I wondered if she was simply not hungry. I wondered if somehow the signals were tangled in her brain and that she wanted to eat but could not respond to the need to eat. I felt helplessness and even impatience again. But then I remembered that she had been patient with me for over fifty years. I could at least be patient with her waiting a few more minutes for her to eat.

March 31, 2006: I am not counting the days any longer, except to count them on the billing from the nursing home. The total days in the nursing home is now nine hundred twenty-six. I have not missed a day, but Edna is not eating for me when I try to feed her lunch. I do not think she even knows that I am there.

April 21, 2006: I find myself slipping deeper and deeper into depression. I still try to feed Edna each day, but she is not responsive and does not even acknowledge my presence. When she does not respond, I feel useless and dispirited.

April 30, 2006: I sit here at home alone again this early Sunday morning. I am still in deep depression. I lay awake with insomnia during the nights. But I am determined not to burden others who may have their own burdens to bear. I am also determined not to take medication for depression or insomnia. This would be a false temporary support. I will continue to draw upon my faith and private prayer that God will help lift me up out of this black hole.

May 20, 2006 was a beautiful spring day outside. I rolled Edna in the wheel chair out into the sunshine. I continued to talk to her as if she heard me, but she was unresponsive. I tried to flex her arms, as I have tried to do on many occasions, but they remained clinched across her chest, as if Death was trying to claim her and take her away from me. I wondered how long we would have the strength to fight these demons of death. I wondered why God lets her die this slow death.

As we see loved ones and friends approach death, we are reminded of our own mortality. We plan our estates, write our wills, leave directions for our funerals, and sometimes even design our head stones. But do we plan for the Life after death?

May 29, 2006. Memorial Day, a day to remember those who have passed through the veil between life and death. But how do we remember those who still remain at the edge of the veil? We try to remember how our loved ones once appeared. We try to forget how they now appear.

Each day of our life should be a Memorial Day: Each day to remember not only those who have gone before us but those still with us: Each day to remember and cherish our loved ones, children, grandchildren, and friends, with hugs, kisses, listening and talking, because soon they will be gone, leaving empty places at the table, empty homes, and empty hearts, with only pictures to remember the happy days of youth long gone.

Although I do not count the days any more, I continue to pray for Edna each day. I continue to visit her each day. I also thank God each day for the strength to continue my daily vigil with her.

I also continue to write this love story. When I started writing this story more than four years ago, I did so as a form of therapy for me and to help others who might experience long term illness in the family. Other than giving a few complimentary copies to family and close friends, I had no desire to have this story copied or published. I continue to write the love story as a very personal and private part of my life. I do not care if it is never published. It may never be finished. I do not know how this story will end. It may end with a simple blank page at the end.

THE FINAL CALL

May 30, 2006

When I wrote the note yesterday, I did not then know what the next day would bring. This next day brought the Final Call. My Loved One passed quietly away in her sleep in the early dawn of this New Day. She passed beyond the veil into eternal rest at a better place with all of the other Angels.

EPILOGUE

September, 2006

The eulogies have been said;
The last song has been sung;
The last note of the music has been played;
The friends have left;
The funeral flowers are gone;
The fall wind blows through the cemetery;
I am alone in this lonely place.

Oh, the Love of my Life, my Sweetheart,
I miss you so much!
How I wish I could still feed you
Bite by bite, or
Touch you again, or even see you;
But now, I weep at your grave;
I have lost you twice;
I pray that God will help me
Find you again some day.

Watercolor by Allen Shoffner
2006

Eternal Peace for
Our Loved One

Printed in the United States
By Bookmasters